MY NUT FREE RECIPE BOOK

BY
KIRSTEN GREENWOOD

MY NUT FREE RECIPE BOOK

Text copyright © 2007 Kirsten Rachel Neill Greenwood

Illustrations copyright © Elaine Durack

First published in Great Britain in 2007

AT Press, 25 Cholmeley Park, London, N6 5EL, UK

A Catalogue record for this book is available from the British Library

ISBN 978-0-9547906-1-5

Designed by Simon Banister
Production by Adrienne Hanratty
Printed and bound in Great Britain by Halstan

Hi, I'm Kirsten...

I have put this book together. The idea
of a nut free recipe book came to me
a couple of years ago because I have
a serious nut allergy, and others with
nut allergies, or any other allergies,
will know how hard it is not being
able to eat food at parties; or looking
at something in the supermarket that looks
delicious, but you can't eat it. Or flicking through
a recipe book where the mouth watering recipes are going to make you
really ill.

Well I knew I couldn't change people having nuts in their party food,
or stop supermarket food from containing nuts, but since I have already
published a book and I was looking for a new idea, this seemed like the
perfect opportunity.

And then I had another idea, I wouldn't just put my own recipes in,
I would ask others as well. So I sent letters out to all my friends and
family asking them to donate a family recipe that they liked, but of
course, it couldn't contain nuts. Before I go on, I would like to thank
everybody who found the time to donate a recipe for this book.

After that, my Mummy, Aunt and I had a long, hard job ahead of us.
We had to proof read the book at least 5 times to check for mistakes.
Recipes from abroad used different measurements and ingredients that
we don't have in this country. Simon Banister, the book's designer, came
up with many different designs for the layout, colour and typeface for

the way the book would look. Elaine Durack, our talented artist, had to draw pictures for every single recipe and it was a hard job looking through them and having to ask her to redo a few of them! Adrienne Hanratty organised the printing of the book for us.

I decided to donate all the money I made from the book to the Anaphylaxis Campaign – a charity that helps people with any serious allergies.

And finally, I have a few more people to thank, but I won't go through all of them, because then the list would be longer than the book itself! But thank you to all the people who made this book happen.

Kirsten Greenwood
December 2006

Contents

▶ Starters

Liz and Sarah's potato wedges   2

Mo-pa's sugar sandwiches by my Great-Grandfather, Mo-pa   3

Irish soda bread by Mrs Hanratty   4

Roast vegetable soup by Mrs Hanratty   5

Simon's trio of creamed mushroom soup   6

Peter Newmark's curried cauliflower soup   7

Great Auntie Margaret's As-you-like-it soup   8

Lisbet's mother's rolls   9

Grandma's soup on a nail   10

Kitchka's savoury fingers   12

▶ Mains

Mette's Danish meatballs   14

Lemon spaghetti for two hungry people by Jan   15

Spaghetti with salmon sauce by Janice and family   16

Linda's spaghetti bolognese   17

Karen's porcupines   18

Yums Yums by Elaine, Linda and Gaby (the dog)   19

Spaghetti with eggs and bacon by Finn Keenan   20

Christian's hamburgers   21

Mash pie by Alexandra (Alex) Legg   22

Emma's quiche   23

Madeleine and Danielle's artichoke gratin   24

Lentils-dhal by Gianni   25

Eggy bread by Katja   26

Taboulé by Hélène   27

Laura's tuna salad   28

The best fried eggs in the world by Vitek   29

Sausages in Yorkshire pudding by Jayne Crease   30

▶ Desserts

Big no-nutty, no-eggy chocolate cake by Solbjørg   32

Gerd's ginger biscuits   33

Maryann's sticky date pudding   34

   with butterscotch sauce by Miss Griffin   35

Custard kisses by Miss Griffin   36

Benedicte's cake with lemon icing   37

Apple cake by Elena   38

Banana yoghurt brûlée by Jo   39

Delicious Christmas stollen by Cornelia   40

Gwen's holiday fruit cake   41

Finn's quick lunch cake   42

Bulgarian cheese pastry (banitsa) by Kitchka, Rosa and Katherine   43

Chocolate biscuit cake by Elizabeth, Adrian, Anna and Jamie   44

Peaches Geneva by Claire   45

Fruit crumble by Marion   46

Emma Wilson's sponge cake   47

Samuel's favourite cake   48

Cheesecake by Anne-Grete   49

Torvestad's chocolate party cake   50

Mummy's pavlova   51

Grandpa's cheesecake   52

Gingerbread men by Apollonia   53

▶ Drinks

Summer surprise by Hannah   56

Funky flamingo by Jessica   57

Fruity flavour by Kirsten   58

Starters

Liz and Sarah's potato wedges

► Preheat oven to 220°C

1. Cut the potatoes in half length ways, and then into long wedges - skins on

2. Par-boil for about 8 mins

3. Drain the potatoes and pour over the oil, herbs and pepper (drain off excess oil)

4. Roast for approx. 30 mins, turning occasionally, until golden brown and crisp!

Mo-pa's sugar sandwiches by my Great-Grandfather, Mo-pa

1. Butter both slices of bread

2. Pour the sugar on to one slice (make sure it has stuck well to the butter)

3. Place the other slice on top

Ingredients:

2 Slices white bread

A little butter

Sugar to taste

Mo-pa would have said:
"This was my favourite
sandwich. I took it to
work every day."

Irish soda bread
by Mrs Hanratty

Equipment:

Sieve

Floured baking tray

▶ Preheat oven to 200°C

1. Sift together the two flours, bicarbonate of soda and cream of tartar
2. Rub in the butter until the mixture looks like fine breadcrumbs
3. Stir in the buttermilk or skimmed milk and mix until a soft dough
4. Put the dough on to a lightly floured work surface and knead until smooth
5. Shape the dough into a round and place on a lightly floured baking tray
6. Cut a cross in the top and sprinkle with a little flour
7. Bake in the oven for 25-30 mins

Ingredients:

225 g Plain wholemeal flour

200 g Plain white flour (allow a little extra for dusting)

½ Teaspoon bicarbonate of soda

½ Teaspoon cream of tartar

25 g Butter

275 ml Buttermilk or skimmed milk

Roast vegetable soup
by Mrs Hanratty

Equipment:
Roasting tin
Large saucepan
Food processor
or blender

Ingredients:
4 Carrots chopped
2 Parsnips chopped
1 Leek chopped
1.2 litres Vegetable
   stock
2 Teaspoons thyme
   leaves
Salt and pepper
Thyme sprigs to
   garnish

▶ Preheat oven to 200°C

1. Put the carrots and parsnips in a roasting tin and season with salt and pepper

2. Roast in the preheated oven for 1 hour or until the vegetables are very soft

3. 20 mins before the vegetables have finished roasting, put the leeks in a large saucepan with the stock and one teaspoon of thyme

4. Cover the pan and simmer for 20 mins

5. When all the vegetables are done, put them into the food processor or blender and blend, adding a little of the stock if needed

6. Transfer the vegetables to the saucepan and season to taste

7. Add the remaining thyme, stir and simmer for 5 mins

▶ Serve garnished with thyme sprigs and crusty bread.

▶ This entire meal (soup and soda bread, page 4) serves: 6

Mrs Hanratty says:
"This is really one of my favourite soups in winter."

Simon's trio of creamed mushroom soup

Equipment:
Frying pan
Saucepan
Blender
Whisk

Ingredients:
65 g Butter
1.5 Litres Boullion
vegan stock (available
at all health food
shops)
50 g Plain flour
Juice of one lemon
350 g Mixed
mushrooms (plain,
chestnut, oyster)
150 ml Double cream
Salt and pepper to
taste

1. Make a stock based rue in the saucepan with 30 g of the butter, the flour and the boullion stock

2. Melt the remaining butter and the lemon juice in the frying pan on a low heat

3. Wash and chop the mushrooms and sauté them in the butter and lemon juice mixture until all the liquid has evaporated

4. Add the cooked mushrooms to the saucepan with the stock mixture and simmer gently for 15 mins

5. Remove ¾ of the soup from the saucepan and liquidize until nearly smooth and then return to the remaining mixture for improved texture and visual appeal

6. Finally, whisk in the double cream and season to taste

▶ Serve with warm crusty bread and butter.

▶ Serves: 6

Peter Newmark's curried cauliflower soup

Equipment:

Frying pan

1. Gently fry the onion and cumin seeds in olive oil until the onion is soft and the seeds pop
2. Add the other spices
3. Stir and fry for 1 min
4. Add the remaining ingredients and simmer until the cauliflower and potato are soft (about 20 mins)

▶ Serves: 4-6

Ingredients:

1 Tablespoon olive oil

1 Onion chopped

1 Teaspoon cumin seeds

1 Teaspoon turmeric

½ Teaspoon paprika

4 Cups vegetable stock

1 Tin tomatoes

1 Medium potato diced

450 g Cauliflower in small florets

Great Auntie Margaret's As-you-like-it soup

Equipment:
2 Large saucepans

Ingredients:
You need plenty of
vegetables, like
potato, onion, leek,
carrot, haricots verts,
runner beans, celery,
parsnip, cabbage,
broccoli, cauliflower,
spinach - whatever
your family likes (at
least 3 cups)
1 or 2 Vegetable stock
cubes
Small tin of baked
beans in tomato
sauce
Approx. 2 cups
macaroni
Your favourite herbs
Some crushed garlic
Parsley and chopped
chives (optional)

1. Cook some macaroni (about two cups should do) according to the instructions on the packet
2. Wash and cut up the vegetables in small pieces, or whatever size you like
3. Put the vegetables into about 2 litres of boiling water - start with the carrots (they take the longest)
4. Boil all the vegetables until just tender, but not too soft
5. Add one or two vegetable stock cubes
6. Add the herbs and garlic
7. Tip in the baked beans and add the macaroni that you have previously cooked
8. Taste and see if you need more vegetable stock cube
9. Add more water if you think you need it
10. Serve with plenty of chopped parsley and perhaps chopped chives in the pan or in the soup plates

▶ Serves: a hungry family

Great Auntie Margaret says: "A hearty vegetable soup for a hungry family."

Lisbet's mother's rolls

Equipment::
Saucepan
Large bowl

▶ Preheat the oven to 180°C

1. Melt the margarine, add milk (or water) and heat until about 37°C (i.e. tepid)

2. Crumble the yeast into the bowl and stir with some of the fluid

3. Add sugar and salt and the rest of the liquid

4. Mix in the flour and knead well, and even out the surface with your hands

5. Cover with cling film or a towel and let the dough rise to about double the size

6. Roll out as a sausage and divide into approx. 20 even sizes and make into rolls

7. Leave to rise for about 15 mins

8. Bake in a preheated oven for about 10 mins top and 10 mins bottom

▶ Makes: approx. 20 rolls

Ingredients:
500 g Plain flour
2.5 dl Milk (or water)
1 Tablespoon sugar
½ Teaspoon salt
40 g Margarine
25 g Fresh (or dried) yeast

Lisbet says: "I enclose my mother, Aud's, recipe for rolls, which I used to love as a child and which we still bake and have every Sunday breakfast."

Grandma's soup on a nail

This is an old Norwegian folk story about a tramp who tricks a mean, old woman into giving him a delicious soup. My Grandma still tells it to me.

The story is "sort of" like a recipe, so just follow along and make the soup as the story goes. But don't put the nail in or you could get hurt!

Once upon a time a poor man knocked on the door of a lonely farmhouse in Norway. A mean old woman lived on the farm. No-one in the nearby village liked her. The woman opened the door and said, "What do you want?" in a snappy voice.

The man said, "I am very hungry. Could I have something to eat?"

The woman replied angrily, "I never give to beggars."

And the man said calmly, "I understand that, but could you make soup on a nail?"

The lady got very curious and asked, "Could you really do that?"

The poor man said, "Certainly, would you like me to show you?"

The lady said "Yes, come in."

As she was a mean lady she thought this was a wonderful idea. So the man said, "Do you have a saucepan?" and the woman said, "Of course."

The next question was, "Could you fill it to the half way point and put in a very good nail?"

When the water was boiling, the man said, "I suppose you don't have a meat bone?"

The woman said, "Of course I have. There is one from yesterday."

Then the man put the bone in the pot. Then he said, "You don't have one or two potatoes, do you?"

And the lady thought, and said, "Yes, I suppose I have."

The man was very grateful. He peeled the potatoes and put them in the pot. Then he said, "I visited your neighbours and they grew some lovely swedes and leeks, but I can see that you don't have any."

The woman, who wanted to be better than the neighbours said, "Of course I have some," and gave him two leeks and half a swede.

The man washed and peeled the vegetables and put them in the pot which was now simmering happily. There was a lovely smell in the kitchen. The man looked around and said, "You wouldn't have a spice cupboard, would you? I would be grateful for just some salt and pepper."

The woman said, angrily, "Of course I have a spice cupboard. I have both salt and pepper and both thyme and mixed herbs."

So the man sprinkled a bit of each on the soup. After a while the man took a spoonful and gave it to the woman to taste. The woman said, in a surprised voice, "It is lovely! I hope you will let me keep the nail!"

The man said, "Of course", and the woman suddenly smiled. "Let us sit down, I have some newly made bread to go with the soup as well as some newly made butter."

She then said to the man, "I think you are a real magician."

Kitchka's savoury fingers

Equipment:
Sieve
Mixing bowl
Baking tin (approx. 33 cm in diameter)
Saucepan
Teacup
Pastry cutter or knife

▶ Preheat oven to 200°C

1. Sieve flour and baking powder in the bowl
2. Make a hole in the middle and pour in ¾ of the beaten egg mixture, all the yoghurt and a little salt
3. Gradually start incorporating some of the surrounding flour
4. Meanwhile, melt the margarine and actually let it come to the boil
5. Take off the heat immediately and pour over the flour which has not yet been mixed together with the egg, etc.
6. Now mix everything together and knead for a few minutes
7. Form a ball and leave covered in the fridge overnight
8. The next day, bring to room temperature
9. Roll the dough a little and fit snugly into a baking tin that has been oiled
10. Cut into fingers using a pastry knife or cutter
11. Brush with the remaining egg and sprinkle with rock salt, cumin or other flavouring
12. Bake for about 30 mins

Ingredients:
250 g Margarine
3 Standard teacups full of plain flour
2 Beaten eggs
1½ Teaspoons baking powder
1½ Teaspoons natural yoghurt
Rock salt, cumin or other flavouring

Mains

Mette's Danish meatballs

1. Mix all the ingredients together – it should not be too dry. If it is, add a little more mineral water
2. Then form the mixture into balls the size of a tablespoon
3. Fry them in the frying pan. When you put them in the pan, flatten them a little with a fork
4. Fry for approx. 5 mins each side, then they should be ready
5. Try one and see if you want them to fry longer

▶ Serve with potatoes or pasta and any sauce you like.

Ingredients:
0.5 kg Minced meat (pork or beef mixture)
1 Egg
1 Small onion
1 Tablespoon flour
1 Tablespoon grated breadcrumbs
1 Splash of sparkling mineral water
Pepper and salt as you want
A little bit of basil or oregano, or both if you like
Olive oil for frying

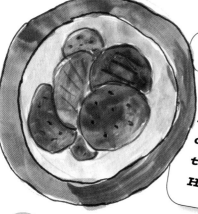

Mette says: "Kristina (my daughter) loves them, and starts eating them when I'm still frying. Just take one on a fork and eat it, that really tastes nice. Her record is 20 at a time!"

14

Lemon spaghetti for two hungry people by Jan

Equipment:

Large saucepan

Mixing bowl

Lemon juicer

1. Put the water on to boil for the pasta

2. While it is heating, mix the juice of the lemon with the same amount of olive oil

3. Add enough grated Parmesan cheese to thicken and lots of ground black pepper

4. When the water boils, throw in the salt, spaghetti and lemon rind cut into fine strips

5. Cook the spaghetti until al dente

6. Drain and mix with the sauce and basil leaves

7. Serve immediately with extra Parmesan (and salad, optional)

Ingredients:

250 g Black spaghetti with squid ink (ordinary spaghetti will also do)

Juice and peel of one unwaxed lemon

Equal quantity of good olive oil

300 g Parmesan cheese, finely grated

A handful of basil leaves, washed and torn into small pieces

Salt and ground black pepper

Jan says: "A very quick, simple dish."

15

Spaghetti with salmon sauce by Janice and family

1. Chop the onion and garlic finely

2. Fry in two tablespoons of olive oil until golden

3. Put the spaghetti in boiling water and cook until al dente (follow instructions on the packet)

4. Open the tin of salmon. Take out any bones and take the skin off (if required)

5. Put the salmon in the saucepan with the garlic and onions

6. Add the tin of tomatoes and the small tin of tomato purée

7. Drain the spaghetti and serve

8. Share the salmon out between four plates

▶ Serves: 4

Equipment:
2 Saucepans

Ingredients:
1 Large tin of salmon (pink or red)
1 Large tin tomatoes
1 Small tin tomato purée
2 Cloves garlic
1 Onion
1 Packet spaghetti (for four people)
Olive oil

Janice says: "Enjoy."

Linda's spaghetti bolognese

Ingredients:

350 g Minced meat

1 Onion

Small tin / box of

  tomato sauce

1 Oxo cube

Salt, pepper, mixed

  herbs

Olive oil

Spaghetti

Grated Parmesan

  cheese

1. Heat up the olive oil in a saucepan and chop up the onion - fry quickly

2. Add the meat and brown it

3. Put in the tomato sauce, oxo cube, salt and pepper and mixed herbs

4. Put in approx. 1/3 the amount of water as tomato sauce

5. Simmer for at least half an hour on a low heat, stirring from time to time

6. Cook up the spaghetti in a separate saucepan following the cooking time on the packet

7. When ready, strain the spaghetti and add the bolognese sauce

8. Mix it up and serve with grated Parmesan cheese on top

▶ Serves: 3

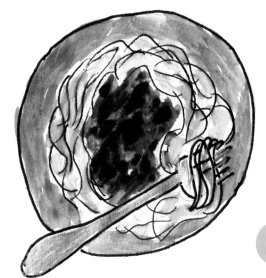

Karen's porcupines

1. Cut the onion into very small pieces
2. Fry in a saucepan with a little olive oil until almost soft
3. Add in the mince and brown it stirring regularly
4. Stir in the tomato purée and about ¼ pint of water
5. Crumble in the oxo cube
6. Add salt and pepper to taste and mixed herbs
7. Simmer gently for 30-45 mins, stirring now and then (add water if the mixture dries out)
8. 20 mins before serving, measure out two mugs full of rice into another saucepan
9. Rinse the rice three times in water
10. Add 2⅛ mugs of water to the rice and bring to the boil
11. Cover and turn heat to the absolute minimum; leave for 16 mins
12. Once the rice is ready, remove from the heat and stir in about $^4/_5$ths of the rice into the meat sauce
13. To serve, use a serving spoon as a mould to create the porcupine mothers and a dessertspoon as a mould to create the porcupine babies
14. Serve with a little of the plain rice and with lambs lettuce – two mothers and three babies per person

Equipment:
2 Saucepans

Ingredients:
½ Onion
Olive oil
500 g Minced meat (beef or lamb)
1 Oxo cube
2 Heaped dessert spoons tomato purée
Salt and pepper
½ Teaspoon mixed herbs
2 Mugs basmati rice
Lambs lettuce or other green vegetables

Karen says: "I invented this dish to tempt my niece, Kirsten, the author!"

Yums Yums by Elaine, Linda and Gaby (the dog)

▶ Preheat oven to a high temperature (approx. 200°C)

1. Chop everything up into little squares (the smaller they are the crisper they'll be)

2. Put in the roasting tray with olive oil and sprinkle some mixed herbs over them

3. Bake them on a high heat for about 30 mins or until they are brown and crispy

4. Serve with anything. Good with chops, steak, sausages, fish, or you can even chop up some bacon to mix in

Ingredients:
Sweet potatoes
Parsnips
Raw beetroot
Ordinary potatoes
Olive oil
Mixed herbs

Elaine, Linda and Gaby say (or woof!): "We lurve this one, they are sooooo nice."

Spaghetti with eggs and bacon by Finn Keenan

1. Bring a large pan of water to the boil

2. In a medium frying pan, heat the oil and sauté the bacon and the garlic until the bacon renders its fat and starts to brown

3. Remove and discard the garlic — keep the bacon hot until needed

4. Add salt and the spaghetti to the boiling water in the saucepan and cook until it is al dente

5. While the pasta is cooking, warm a large serving bowl and break the eggs into it

6. Beat in the grated Parmesan cheese with a fork and season with salt and pepper

7. As soon as the pasta is done, drain it quickly and mix it into the egg mixture

8. Pour on the hot bacon and its fat and stir well

9. The heat from the pasta, bacon and bacon fat will cook the eggs

10. Serve immediately

Equipment:
Saucepan
Medium frying pan
Large serving bowl

Ingredients:
2 Tablespoons olive oil
Generous half cup of bacon cut into matchsticks
1 Clove garlic — crushed
450 g Spaghetti
3 Eggs at room temperature
¾ Cup freshly grated Parmesan cheese
Salt and freshly ground black pepper

Finn says: "Yum."

Christian's hamburgers

Equipment:
Mixing bowl
Barbeque or grill

Ingredients:
500 g Minced meat
Hamburger buns
1 Egg per 500 g of
 minced meat
Handful of sliced
 pickled cucumber,
 finely chopped
A small portion of
 pickled cucumber
 liquid (i.e. one
 tablespoon)
A small portion of
 good barbeque spice
 (i.e. one teaspoon)
A small portion of
 good barbeque sauce
 (i.e. one tablespoon)

1. Mix all the hamburger ingredients together by hand
2. If you feel the consistency is a little liquidy for your taste, add some flour while mixing. Otherwise the hamburgers may fall apart especially when grilling
3. Separate the mixture into handful size portions by hand
4. Flatten them slightly by hand and fry for 3-5 mins before turning once (if you want the hamburgers well done, cook for 1-2 mins more each side)
5. Serve in a bun with all your favourite pickings, such as salad, tomato, pickled or plain cucumber, corn, mustard, mayonnaise, and/or French fries

▶ Serves: 4-5

Mash pie
by Alexandra (Alex) Legg

▶ Preheat the oven to 180°C

1. Peel and cut the potatoes

2. Boil until cooked (15-20 mins)

3. Mash with plenty of butter and a little milk until smooth and creamy

4. Add salt and pepper to taste

5. Cook the sausages in the oven for about 20 mins, until they are golden brown

6. Heat the peas or beans (in the microwave would do)

Equipment:
Saucepan
Roasting tray
Serving plate

Ingredients:
Potatoes
Butter
Salt and pepper
Milk
Peas or baked beans
Cocktail sausages

▶ Assemble your pie:

1. Place the peas or beans on a serving plate and spread out

2. Using a large spoon, put the mash on top

3. Now stick the sausages into the mash

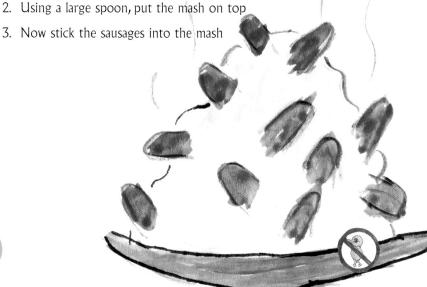

Emma's quiche

- Preheat the oven to 200°C

- Pastry:

1. Mix cookeen and flour by chopping up finely into small pieces

2. Add the salt and lemon juice and mix with enough water to make a dough

3. Roll and put into a greased quiche dish

- Quiche:

1. Take a fork and prick the bottom of the pastry all over

2. Put a thin layer of mustard all over the bottom of the pastry

3. Put tuna all over in little chunks

4. In a separate bowl, mix the three eggs with two dessertspoonfuls of thick, low-fat crème fraîche

5. Pour the mixture over the tuna

6. Spread grated emmenthal over the mixture until it is completely covered

7. Optional sliced tomatoes to decorate

8. Cook in the oven for 30 mins

9. Take it out, cut it and then eat it

Equipment:
Quiche dish
Greaseproof paper
Mixing bowl

Pastry Ingredients:
125 g Cookeen
125 g Flour
Pinch of salt
Good squirt of lemon
Water to mix
Alternatively, buy ready made nut-free pastry

Quiche Ingredients:
Dijon mustard (check it is nut free! If not, use another type of mustard)
Big tin of tuna
3 Eggs
2 Dessertspoons thick low-fat crème fraîche
Grated emmenthal
Sliced tomatoes (optional)

Madeleine and Danielle's artichoke gratin

Equipment:

2 Saucepans

Oven-proof dish

▶ Preheat oven to 200°C

Ingredients:

1 kg Frozen (or tinned) artichoke hearts

1 litre Béchamel sauce

Curry powder

Salt and pepper

Gruyère cheese

Parmesan cheese (optional)

1. Cook the artichokes in salted boiling water until they are tender (test to see)

2. Drain the artichokes

3. Prepare a Béchamel sauce that is quite liquid

4. Add curry powder (to taste) and salt and pepper

5. Melt the Gruyère cheese on top

6. Cut the artichokes up a bit and put them into an oven-proof dish

7. Pour the sauce over the artichokes

8. Sprinkle a little grated Parmesan over the top if required

9. Put in the oven for about 35-40 mins

▶ Serves: 8-10

Lentils-dhal by Gianni

1. Heat the ol in a deep pan
2. Once the oil is really hot, add the cumin seeds and let them splutter
3. Then add the chopped up onion and stir
4. Let the onion sweat and then add the ginger and garlic that has been puréed, stir well
5. Now add the tomato and turmeric powder, stir well
6. Finally add the lentils (washed dhal)
7. Cover the ingredients with enough water so that you have ½ inch of water above
8. Now add the salt and stir thoroughly
9. Wait until the water comes to the boil. You should be on a high heat
10. Once the water comes to the boil, reduce the heat right down
11. Cover and let it cook for 20-25 mins
12. Check if you like in between and stir occasionally
13. If you have not added enough water earlier, you may do so later. The thickness of the dhal depends on how much water is added

► Serve with some salad and basmati rice or with Indian breads (naans, chapatis or parathas). Interestingly, it tastes just as good with bread and butter! Very nutritious and high in protein.

Ingredients:

1 Cup lentils (Masoor Dhal, wash well) put aside

1 Teaspoon cumin seeds

2 Tablespoons vegetable or olive oil

1 Medium sized onion chopped up small

1 Medium/large tomato chopped up small

3 Cloves garlic puréed

1 Inch Ginger puréed

1 Teaspoon turmeric powder (haldi)

1 Teaspoon salt (depending on taste)

25

Eggy bread by Katja

1. Crack the egg into the cup or bowl

2. Beat until ready

3. Ask an adult to turn on the cooker/ stove and place the frying pan on top

4. Pour the egg into the frying pan – it should sizzle a bit

5. Put the bread in the frying pan on top of the egg

6. Wait 10 secs or a little more then flip over with the spatula and wait until golden brown

7. Turn off the cooker and take out the eggy bread and put on a plate

Equipment:
One adult
Cup or bowl
Egg beater/fork
Frying pan
Spatula

Ingredients:
Bread
1 Egg

Taboulé by Hélène

Equipment:
Large bowl
Blender

Ingredients:
200-250 g Couscous
4 Tomatoes
Bunch of parsley or
   coriander
1 Large lemon
4 Spring onions
1 Clove garlic
3 Tablespoons olive oil
Salt and pepper

1. Put the couscous in a bowl and cover with cold water (one finger high of water extra on top) and let it rest for 1 hour

2. The couscous will absorb all the water. If there is still some water left after 1 hour, the couscous can be pressed and the water extracted

3. Cut the tomatoes in two, scoop out the pips and inside flesh, etc., and cut into small squares

4. Mix the tomato squares into the couscous

5. Slice the spring onions

6. Press the garlic

Hélène says: "A taboulé is best eaten cold. Season again to taste if need be before serving."

7. Put the tomato remnants (pips and flesh), herbs (take off some of the stalks), the spring onions and the garlic into a blender and chop it all finely

8. Mix the couscous with the tomato/herb mixture

9. Add the olive oil, lemon juice and salt and pepper to taste and mix very thoroughly with forks

10. Store in the fridge for at least 2 hours so that the marinade flavours have time to develop

▶ Serves: 6+

27

Laura's tuna salad

1. Take a saucepan and wash the rice three times before cooking it
2. When the rice is cooked, strain and leave it to cool
3. Take another saucepan and boil the eggs
4. When hard boiled leave the eggs in cold water
5. Meanwhile cut the tomatoes into small pieces and open the tin of tuna which should be crushed into small pieces
6. Then put it all in the salad bowl
7. When the rice is cold, put it in with the tuna and tomatoes
8. When the eggs are cold, peel the shells and cut them into small pieces and put them in with the rest of the ingredients
9. Pour in the olive oil and vinegar
10. Toss with salad servers

Ingredients:
Rice
Tomatoes (one for each person)
Eggs (one for each person)
1 Large tin of tuna
Olive oil
Vinegar

Kirsten says: "I ADORE this salad!"

The best fried eggs in the world by Vitek

Equipment:
Bowl
1 Long handled teaspoon
Frying pan

Ingredients:
2 Good quality free-range eggs
40 g Good salted butter
1 Teaspoon vegetable oil
1 Tablespoon white wine vinegar
Salt and pepper

1. Crack open the two eggs and put into a bowl making sure you don't crack the yolk
2. Then add a pinch of salt and pepper
3. Take the butter and put it in the frying pan
4. Add the vegetable oil and heat until they start to go brown
5. Pour the eggs into the frying pan
6. Use the spoon to pour the butter and oil over the eggs
7. Pour away some of the butter and oil, but don't let your eggs get hard – they will go dark
8. Put the eggs on a plate
9. Put the vinegar in the frying pan and let it boil and reduce until there is only a little left
10. Pour the vinegar over your eggs and enjoy it

Sausages in Yorkshire pudding by Jayne Crease

Equipment:

Sieve

Bowl

Whisk

Muffin tray

▶ Preheat oven to 220°C

1. Sieve the flour and salt into a bowl and make a hole in the centre (for the eggs)

2. Add the eggs one by one

3. Whisk the milk into the eggs and flour until you have a smooth batter with no lumps

Ingredients:

A pinch of salt

3 Eggs

250 ml Milk

150 g Plain flour

6 Sausages cut in half

4 Tablespoons vegetable oil

4. Use the muffin tray and add one teaspoon of oil in each hole and put into the oven for 3 mins

5. Take the hot muffin tray out of the oven and add half a sausage to each hole

6. Put back in the oven for 8 mins

7. Take the muffin tray out of the oven and half fill each hole with batter and cook for 18-20 mins

▶ Makes: 12

Desserts

Big no-nutty, no-eggy chocolate cake by Solbjørg

▶ Preheat oven to 200°C

▶ Cake:

1. Mix everything together in a bowl or blender until it is smooth, but not longer

2. Pour into a baking tin lined with greaseproof paper

3. Cook in the oven for 30 mins

▶ Icing:

1. Mix everything together in a bowl

2. Spread on top of the cake, when it has cooled to room temperature

Solbjørg says: "My favourite recipe is for a moist, delicious chocolate cake. The recipe does not involve eggs either. I hope you enjoy it."

Equipment:
Small saucepan
Bowl or blender
Large square baking tin
Greaseproof paper
Spatula

Cake Ingredients:
150 g Melted butter – not too hot
6 dl Sugar
10 dl Flour
1 Tablespoon baking soda
6-8 Tablespoons strong drinking chocolate powder
7½ dl Sour milk

Icing Ingredients:
100 g Melted butter – not too hot
300 g Icing Sugar
4 Tablespoons strong drinking chocolate powder
3 Teaspoons vanilla sugar
2 Tablespoons strong coffee

Gerd's ginger biscuits

▶ Preheat oven to 180°C

1. Warm the syrup and margarine in a saucepan until melted
2. Mix all the other ingredients in a bowl
3. Add in the syrup and margarine and make into a dough
4. Roll into little balls and place on greaseproof paper on a baking tray
5. Press a flat fork lightly into the top of each ball to make a mark of the prongs
6. Bake in the oven for 10-15 mins until lightly brown

Equipment:
Small saucepan
Bowl
Baking tray
Greaseproof paper

Ingredients:
2 dl White flour
2 Tablespoons margarine
½ Tablespoon sugar
⅛ Teaspoon pepper
⅛ Teaspoon ground cloves
¼ Teaspoon ground ginger
1 Teaspoon baking powder
¼ Teaspoon cream of tartar
3 Tablespoons warm syrup
1 Tablespoon cream

Maryann's sticky date pudding

▶ Preheat oven to moderate temperature (170-180°C)

▶ Sticky date pudding:

1. Grease a deep 20 cm round cake tin
2. Line with greaseproof paper
3. Combine the dates and water in a pan, bring to the boil and then immediately remove from the heat
4. Stir in the soda and allow to stand for 5 mins
5. Blend or process the date mixture with the butter and sugar until almost smooth
6. Add the eggs and flour
7. Blend or process until just combined
8. Pour the mixture into the prepared cake tin

Sticky Date Pudding Ingredients:

1¼ Cups seeded dates
1¼ Cups boiling water
1 Teaspoon baking soda
60 g Chopped butter
¾ Cup firmly packed brown sugar
2 Eggs
1 Cup self-raising flour

9. Bake for approx. 45 mins or until cooked through. Cover with foil during baking if getting too brown
10. Stand the pudding for 10 mins before turning out of the tin
11. Serve with butterscotch sauce poured over the top

with butterscotch sauce
by Miss Griffin

- ▶ Butterscotch sauce:
1. Combine ingredients in a medium pan
2. Stir over a low heat until the sugar is dissolved and the butter melted

Tip: pudding and sauce can be made a day ahead

Butterscotch Sauce Ingredients:

1 Cup firmly packed brown sugar

300 ml Cream

200 g Butter

Custard kisses
by Miss Griffin

▶ Preheat oven to 150°C

1. Warm butter until soft (not melted)
2. Mix in a large bowl with icing sugar and vanilla until creamy
3. Sieve in the flour, custard powder and baking powder
4. Mix well squeezing the dough together by hand and adding some milk if dry
5. Roll into approx. 40 small balls and flatten on the greased baking tray with a floured fork
6. Bake for 12 mins until biscuits feel firm but not browned
7. Leave to cool
8. Mix all the icing ingredients together and ice the biscuits and then join them together

Biscuit Ingredients:
175 g Butter
1 Cup icing sugar
1 Teaspoon vanilla
1½ Cups flour
½ Cup custard powder
1 Teaspoon baking powder

Icing Ingredients:
2 Tablespoons butter
½ Cup icing sugar
1 Tablespoon custard powder
Vanilla essence

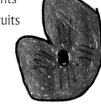

Benedicte's cake with lemon icing

► Preheat oven to 200°C

► Cake:

1. Mix together the butter and sugar

2. Add the flour, baking powder and milk

3. Separate the eggs

4. Add the yolk first and then beat the egg white and add at the end

5. Take the lemon, grate the peel and add this to the cake batter

6. Put the batter into a greased cake tin

7. Bake in the oven for approx. 40 mins

8. Cool down and make the icing

Cake Ingredients:
1 Cup butter

2 Cups sugar

3 Cups flour

2 Teaspoons baking powder

1 Cup milk

3 Eggs

Grated rind from one lemon

► Lemon icing:

1. Sift the icing sugar into a bowl

2. Mix in the lemon juice gradually, until a thick liquid consistency. Add a little water if necessary

Lemon Icing Ingredients:
Juice from one lemon

225 g Icing sugar

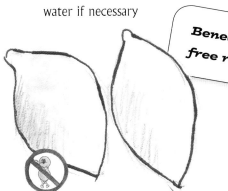

Benedicte says: "This is a nut-free recipe from my mother."

Apple cake by Elena

Equipment:
Cake tin (20-23 cm)
Greaseproof paper
Blender

► Preheat oven to 200°C

1. Mix the eggs and sugar together and add the flour
2. Then add the baking soda (the dough should look like thick cream)
3. Grease and line the baking tin with greaseproof paper
4. Cut the apples into 2-3 cm pieces and add into the cake tin
5. Pour the dough over and let it stand a bit
6. Bake in the oven for about 30-40 mins until ready (measured by poking a cocktail stick into the cake and seeing if it is dry and ready when you bring it out)

Ingredients:
3 Eggs
½ Cup sugar
⅔ Cup flour
½ Teaspoon baking soda
3 Green apples

Elena says: "The apple cake can be served with whipped cream or ice cream."

Banana yoghurt brûlée
by Jo

Equipment:

2 Ramekin dishes
(more if needed)

▶ Preheat grill

1. Slice the banana into the base of the ramekin dishes

2. Spoon the yoghurt on top and level it out leaving about 5 mm at the top of each ramekin dish

3. Scatter the sugar on top of the yoghurt

4. Place the dishes under a hot grill until the sugar is bubbling all over (depending on your grill, this can happen quite fast, so it's best to keep your eye on it)

5. Carefully remove the hot dishes and allow to stand for 2-3 mins to allow the sugar to harden before serving

Ingredients:

½ Banana
1 Small pot Greek yoghurt
2-3 Teaspoons demerara sugar

Jo says: "A quick and easy, but lovely, pudding."

Delicious Christmas stollen by Cornelia

Equipment:
Large bowl
Greased baking tray

▶ Preheat oven to 200°C

1. Mix the cornflour, flour, baking powder, sugar, eggs and drained quark

2. Wash the raisins and currants with hot water and mix in together with the vanilla flavour, mixed peel and lemon juice

3. Cut 200 g of cold butter into flakes and knead in

4. Roll out the dough into a rectangular shape with one side thicker than the opposite one

5. Put the stollen on to a greased baking tray and bake for 1 hour until golden brown (you may have to cover with baking paper towards the end to avoid burning)

6. When done, brush with melted butter while still hot and dust with a thick layer of icing sugar

7. When it has cooled, put it in a tin or wrap in aluminium foil and store in a cool, dry place for at least one week for a better taste

Ingredients:
100 g Cornflour
500 g Flour
2½ Teaspoons baking powder
200 g Sugar
3 Eggs
250 g Quark
(alternatively 125 g fromage frais and 125 g ricotta cheese)
200 g Raisins
200 g Dried currants
100 g Mixed peel
Vanilla flavour to taste
1 Tablespoon lemon juice
200 g Cold butter
100 g Melted butter
125 g Icing sugar

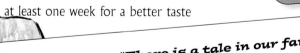

Cornelia says: "There is a tale in our family that an aunt once completely forgot about her Christmas stollen and only found it when she was doing her Spring clean the following Easter. Allegedly, the family never before or after enjoyed a stollen as much as this one!"

Gwen's holiday fruit cake

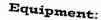

Equipment:
Saucepan
Bowl
Round cake tin
(20 cm)

Ingredients:
1 Can (300 ml)
  condensed milk
1¼ Cups water
250 g Butter
500 g Mixed dried
  fruit
½ Cup glacé cherries
Grated rind of one
  orange
2 Cups plain flour
1 Teaspoon vanilla
  essence
½ Teaspoon
  bicarbonate of soda
½ Teaspoon salt

▶ Preheat oven to moderately slow temperature (170-180°C)

1. Put into the saucepan the condensed milk, water, butter, fruits and orange rind

2. Stir over a low heat for 3-5 mins

3. Remove from the heat and put aside for 10 mins

4. Add the vanilla essence

5. Sift together the flour, bicarbonate of soda and salt in a bowl

6. Add to the warm fruit mixture and combine thoroughly

7. Spoon into a well greased 20 cm round cake tin

8. Bake in a moderately slow oven for 1¼ hours or until done when tested

9. Remove from the oven. Leave for 10 mins before turning out on to a cake rack

Gwen says: "This is a real favourite of mine and I have been making it for the last 20 or so years."

41

Finn's quick lunch cake

▶ Preheat oven to 170°C

▶ Cake:

1. Melt the margarine and let it cool

2. Mix in with the rest of the ingredients with an electric whisk

3. Put in a cake tin lined with greaseproof paper

4. Cook on the lowest shelf in the oven for 20-25 mins

5. Take out and leave to cool on a rack

▶ Icing:

1. Mix all the ingredients together and pour over the cake

2. Decorate the cake with whatever you have available

Equipment:
Saucepan
Electric whisk
Cake tin (20 x 33 cm)
Greaseproof paper

Cake Ingredients:
300 g Margarine
4 Eggs
270 g Sugar
1½ Teaspoons vanilla sugar
4 Dessertspoons unsweetened cocoa powder (not drinking chocolate)
300 g White flour
3 Teaspoons baking powder
2 dl Milk

Icing Ingredients:
125 g Margarine
250 g Icing sugar
2 Teaspoons vanilla sugar
1¼ Dessertspoons unsweetened cocoa powder
3 Dessertspoons coffee (optional)

Bulgarian cheese pastry (banitsa) by Kitchka, Rosa and Katherine

► Preheat oven to 190°C

1. Melt the butter / margarine

2. Crumble the cheese

3. Whisk the eggs and mix with the cheese, leaving a little egg for glazing

4. Add a couple of spoonfuls of yoghurt

5. Grease the baking tray and start by laying a sheet of filo pastry on the base. It is not necessary to stretch the sheet

6. Brush the sheet with the melted butter

7. Follow with another sheet, brush with butter and spread on some of the cheese mixture

8. Continue until all the pastry and cheese mixture have been used up, ending with a sheet of filo pastry

9. Brush with butter, followed by the left-over beaten egg

10. Cut into squares

11. For a creamier, richer banitsa, whisk an egg with some plain yoghurt and pour over the banitsa making sure some goes in the gaps between the squares

12. Put in the oven. After about 10 mins, turn the heat down to 175°C and continue baking for about 20 mins or until golden

13. After taking out of the oven, cover with a clean cloth for a few minutes before serving. It is also good eaten cold or reheated for breakfast the following morning

43

Chocolate biscuit cake by Elizabeth, Adrian, Anna and Jamie

Equipment:

Saucepan

Flat cake tin

1. Melt together the margarine, cocoa and syrup over a gentle heat

2. Once all mixed together, add the egg, stirring all the time

3. Heat until the mixture thickens slightly with the egg, but NOT to boiling point

4. Stir in the biscuits

5. Press into a flat tin then cool

6. Melt the chocolate and spread over the top

▶ This is such a more-ish recipe that the above quantities are never enough! Try quadrupling it and freezing some once it's made and cut up

Ingredients:

225 g Broken biscuits (e.g. digestive, malted milk, rich tea)

110 g Margarine

2 Tablespoons cocoa

2 Tablespoons golden syrup

1 Beaten egg

110 g Chocolate (milk or dark, or a mixture)

The Juffs family say: "This is our favourite of all favourite cake recipes, which we all like to have a go at making. It's absolutely scrummy."

44

Peaches Geneva by Claire

Equipment:
Baking tray or oven-proof dish

Ingredients:
4 Ripe peaches
Tub of mascarpone cheese
Demerara sugar

▶ Medium to high grill

1. Halve and stone the peaches
2. Place on a baking tray or in a greased oven-proof dish
3. Sprinkle each half generously with sugar
4. Grill (medium to high) for 6 mins
5. Put a dessertspoon full of mascarpone cheese on top of each peach and sprinkle another generous dose of sugar on top
6. Grill (medium to high) for a further 6 mins or until the sugar is melting and browning
7. Serve immediately

▶ Serves: 4

Claire says: "This recipe was served to us by friends who were living in Geneva at the time, and lodged in our minds as Peaches Geneva! Quite delicious."

Fruit crumble by Marion

Equipment:
Bowl
Oven-proof dish

▶ Preheat oven to moderate (170-180°C)

1. Rub flour and crumbs together with the other crumble ingredients
2. Cover the bottom of an oven-proof dish with the fruit and sprinkle some sugar on the top
3. Then pour the crumble mixture over the fruit
4. Bake in the oven until the fruit is cooked

Ingredients:
175 g Mixed plain flour and left over crumbs from cornflakes or bran flakes
110 g Margarine or butter
110 g Sugar (golden if you have it)
Pinch of salt
Fruit e.g. apples, plums, blackcurrants, gooseberries or whatever is available

Emma Wilson's sponge cake

▶ Preheat oven to 180°C

1. Whisk together the butter and sugar
2. Add each egg with a tablespoon of flour, one at a time, and mix well
3. Add the remaining flour, salt and water and mix well
4. Grease the sandwich tins with a little butter and line the bottom of the tins with greaseproof paper
5. Divide the mixture between the tins and bake in the oven until ready
6. When baked, transfer the sponges on to a cooling tray and leave until cool
7. Spread a generous layer of jam on to one sponge. Place the other on top
8. Sprinkle some sieved icing sugar on top (or ice if preferred)

Equipment:
2 Sandwich tins (17.5 cm)
1 Sheet greaseproof paper cut into the shape of the sandwich tins
Cooling rack
Electric mixer
Bowl

Ingredients:
225 g Butter or margarine
225 g Caster sugar
4 Eggs
225 g Self-raising flour
Pinch of salt
1 Tablespoon of warm water
Strawberry jam (use other flavours if preferred)
Icing sugar

Samuel's favourite cake

► Preheat oven to 180°C

1. Mix everything together with an electric mixer all at once for about 3 mins or until smooth
2. Pour into the cake tin and bake for about 40 mins

Equipment:

Electric mixer
Greased cake tin

Ingredients:

1 Cup sour cream
1 Cup caster sugar
1 Cup self-raising flour
2 Eggs
Grated rind of one lemon

Samuel says: "Easy peasy!"

Cheesecake by Anne-Grete

1. Mix the lemon jelly with 2 dl hot water and then cool

2. Whisk the cream until stiff and then stir into the jelly and mix well together

3. Break the digestive biscuits into crumbs and mix with the melted butter

4. Put the biscuits on the bottom of the dish

5. Mix all the cake ingredients together and pour over the biscuits and put the cheesecake into the fridge to set

Equipment:
Bowl

Whisk

Saucepan

Quiche dish

Base Ingredients:
1 Packet digestive biscuits

200 g Melted butter

Cake Ingredients:
1 Packet Philadelphia cream cheese

1 Packet lemon jelly

2 dl hot water

3 dl Whipping cream

3 dl Light crème fraîche

120 g Icing sugar

1 Teaspoon water

Torvestad's chocolate party cake

Equipment:
Round cake tin (25 cm)
Saucepan
Greaseproof paper
Electric mixer

- ▶ Preheat oven to 180°C

- ▶ Cake:

1. Grease the round cake tin
2. Melt the cooking chocolate and the margarine in the saucepan
3. Add the coffee and let it cool
4. Whisk the eggs and the sugar together into a light mixture
5. Sieve the flour and baking powder into this mixture
6. Stir in the cooled chocolate sauce and pour the cake mixture into the cake tin
7. Bake for about 40 mins
8. Let the cake rest a bit before removing carefully from the tin
9. When the cake has cooled, make the icing

- ▶ Icing:

1. Carefully stir the icing sugar and butter (or margarine) together with one egg to make a smooth mix
2. Melt the chocolate and water and stir this in
3. Spread the icing over the cake
4. The cake can also be cut in half and filled in the middle if you want

Cake Ingredients:
125 g Cooking
  chocolate
125 g Margarine
1½ dl Strong coffee
4 Big or 5 small eggs
3 dl Sugar
2 dl Flour
2 Teaspoons baking
  powder

Icing Ingredients:
2½ dl Icing sugar
75 g Butter or
  margarine
1 Egg
125 g Cooking
  chocolate
2 Tablespoons water

50

Mummy's pavlova

Equipment:
Electric whisk
Bowl
Greaseproof paper
Baking tray

Ingredients:
3 Egg whites
Pinch of salt
175 g Caster sugar
1 Teaspoon cornflour
1 Teaspoon white wine
    vinegar
½ Teaspoon vanilla
    essence
A little olive oil
Fresh raspberries,
    strawberries and blue-
    berries (or other fresh
    fruit of your choice)

► Preheat oven to 150°C

1. Separate the eggs and put the egg whites in a bowl (you don't use the yolks in this recipe)

2. Whisk the egg whites and salt until completely stiff (when you turn the bowl upside down the egg whites must not move)

3. Add half the sugar and whisk for a few seconds more

4. Add the cornflour, vinegar and vanilla and the rest of the sugar and whisk for a few seconds more

5. Place a piece of greaseproof paper on to the baking tray and pour a little olive oil on to the top of the paper

6. Pour the mixture on to the olive oil and place in the oven for 40-45 mins or until pale brown

7. Take out of the oven and turn the pavlova over, so the flat surface is facing upwards

8. When cool, put the fresh fruit on the pavlova just before serving

Mummy says: "Kirsten loves my pavlova – it is an easy and delicious party dessert."

Grandpa's cheesecake

► Base:

1. Melt the butter in a saucepan
2. Break the biscuits into crumbs using the food processor
3. Add the butter to the biscuits and spread out evenly to cover the base of the greased quiche dish

► Cheesecake:

1. Clean out the food processor, and then whisk together the Philadelphia cream cheese, condensed milk, lemon juice and vanilla essence. Once these are all mixed together, it should make a thick, creamy mixture
2. Pour the mixture on to the biscuit base and with a spoon, make a light dent in the centre so the pie filling does not overflow
3. Pour the pie filling on the top
4. Please note, this cheese cake is not cooked

Equipment:
Quiche dish
Bowl
Food processor

Base Ingredients:
1 Packet digestive biscuits
3 oz Butter

Cheesecake Ingredients:
3 Small packets Philadelphia cream cheese
1 Small tin condensed milk
Juice of three lemons
½ Teaspoon vanilla essence
1 Tin fruit pie filling (we use cherry pie filling)

Grandpa says: "This is my favourite and I'm sure you'll agree if you taste it too."

Gingerbread men
by Apollonia

▶ Preheat oven to 200°C

1. Put everything into the food processor
2. Once everything is mixed together, take it out of the mixer and make it into one big ball
3. Put the ball into a plastic bag and leave it in the fridge for 1 hour
4. Take it out of the fridge and roll it out flat and cut out (or create) your own shapes
5. Dust the baking trays with flour
6. Place your gingerbread men on the baking trays and bake for 12-15 mins in the centre of the oven

Equipment:
Food processor
Plastic bag
Baking trays

Ingredients:
90 g Margarine
275 g Clear honey
115 g Caster sugar
1½ Teaspoons ground ginger
¼ Teaspoon ground cinnamon
7 g Cocoa powder
675 g Plain flour
1 Teaspoon bicarbonate of soda
Pinch of salt
2 Eggs

Drinks

Summer surprise
by Hannah

1. Put the fruit in the mixer
2. Pour in the milk
3. Mix until smooth
4. Pour yourself some

Equipment:

Mixer or blender

Ingredients:

1 Cup mixed fruit

1 Cup milk

Hannah says: "Very nice in summer."

Funky flamingo by Jessica

Equipment:
Mixer or blender

1. First cut up the strawberries and put them in the mixer

2. Then cut up the mango and put it in the mixer

3. Then pour in the vanilla essence

4. Pour out a dessertspoon of double cream. Make sure it is a dessertspoon – no more, no less!

5. Put on the blender lid and mix it for about 20 secs, but check it after 10 secs

6. Add the ice cubes

7. Now it's your turn to taste and that's the funky flamingo

Ingredients:
½ Mango
15-20 Strawberries
½ Teaspoon vanilla essence
1 Dessertspoon double cream
15–20 Ice cubes

Fruity flavour
by Kirsten

1. Wash the fruit and put it into the blender
2. Add the cranberry juice
3. Blend together
4. Pour into the jug and leave in the fridge until you want to drink it

Equipment:
Blender
Large jug

Ingredients:
1 Banana
Strawberries
Raspberries
Cranberry juice

Kirsten says: "I felt this recipe was mine completely since I invented it. It is so delicious that I couldn't leave it out of my own book!"